WHATEVER IT TAKES.

Lester Love

WHATEVER IT TAKES.

Lester Love

The Love Group
New Orleans, LA 70118

Whatever It Takes.
ISBN 978-0-615-56169-1

Design and layout:
Benjamin Clay, Studio 8 Design, New Orleans, LA

Printed in the United States of America
© 2016 by The Love Group, LLC

The Love Group, LLC
P.O. Box 740249
New Orleans, LA 70174
346.200.5683
info@lesterlove.com

DEDICATION

This book is dedicated to the pastors and leaders that allowed me to serve them. It is those opportunities that afford me the ability to impart to others. My hope is that as a result of my mistakes, they will be wiser.

To Fran, Joy, Faith and Angel: Thank you for always supporting and encouraging my gift of servanthood.

To The City of Love: Thank you for sharing me with the world – serving you brings me absolute joy. You make servanthood easy!

CONTENTS

THE MODEL SERVANT
Standing in the Shadows...

Servanthood has become a forgotten art and, yes, it is an art. The person who accepts the responsibility to serve and is effective in serving is always unique. A person with a servant's mindset is totally unlike the world and its mindset. This person is actually the most Christ-like person in the room. Some people don't have it, while others will learn it or don't want it. Yet, some people are born with it.

To the world, the entire concept of servanthood may be considered tired, worn out, or it defies logic, unless there is some obvious underlying motive. Even though those who work as servants in the commercial arena are compensated, i.e. maids, nannies, personal attendants, executive assistants, etc., if you take away their paychecks, I am afraid that their loyalties will stray. Very few people are willing to serve simply because they love to serve.

Much of this attitude, however, may be attributed to a quest and natural egotistical desire to be the person at the top. There's nothing wrong with that opportunistic view, except that the way to the king's chambers has always been through the servants' quarters. Any attempts to avoid the process and navigate outside of those prescribed parameters have proven both disastrous and painful.

Too many people want a ministry but are not willing to minister. This was the basis of what Jesus said to His disciples in His teaching on servanthood.[1] His conclusion was that if they were going to be like Jesus, they would have to commit to becoming a servant, like Jesus. Jesus called His disciples to become servants because He was a servant. If they were going to carry out the work of evangelism in the entire world, there had to be an identifying attribute that linked each of them to both His personality and His purpose.

The measure of true greatness, then, lies in possessing the attitude of a servant. This kind of posturing does not generally allow you to get much public recognition, but I have found that God will give you fringe benefits as a humble servant that the world would never offer nor could afford.

The apostle, Paul, went through great pains to remind those in church leadership that the teachings of Jesus Christ in regards to the role of a servant had not changed since He spoke to them. There is often the tendency to ascribe meanings

---

[1] **Matthew 23:11**

to the teachings of Jesus that suggest that there is no current relevance, but there are some specific things embedded in this text from Paul's letter to the church at Philippi which lend themselves to the enhancement of greatness, particularly for those who diligently followed these principles.

There are some considerations, which I refer to as part of a blueprint for designing a life in servanthood consistent with the teachings of Christ. We always have to be careful about the examples that we use, if we use secular comparisons. While they may prove acceptable in the short run, they can lose validity when dealing with the sacred. This book emphasizes, and is grounded in, the sacred. If the secular system can identify with any of them, that's good, but our intent is to clearly define servanthood in the context of the teachings of Christ and how they were applied to the New Testament church. The inference is that the contemporary Christian church and its ministries should mirror the New Testament church as closely as possible. Both the resemblance and the identity should be evident, even to the casual observer.

We have identified five (5) aspects of servanthood that are common among those whose calling is in this area. A calling is an anointing for purpose. It means that a person has been set aside and empowered by someone greater than himself for that purpose. There may be other things that can be done on the Kingdom agenda, but a calling is that which a person has been anointed to do, and cannot be ignored, changed, denigrated or marginalized. It has to happen. Even if the person attempts to divert from the execution and demonstration of a calling, it will still go into effect. He may struggle with it, but the assignment is irrevocable.

I am reminded of the Old Testament leader, Moses, who was anointed to lead Israel out of captivity in Egypt. Moses came up with all kinds of exceptions to his calling, but God agreed to none of them.

None of them changed the direction of what God intended as his destiny and purpose. Even his successor, Joshua, had second thoughts about his leadership purpose, but God provided reassurance to him that his designation was real. Elisha was called to serve Elijah and Peter was anointed to serve Jesus. There is no escaping God's anointing for service.

I have to make it clear that I am writing from the standpoint of having been a servant, and I have taken pride in being known from coast to coast as a servant to Bishop Paul S. Morton, Sr. It was not something that I fell into. I am inclined to believe that I was destined for that role and my willing acceptance of that charge to serve him has influenced any measure of success that I have attained. For some reason, it never entered my mind that the position of servant was unduly thrust upon me. Instead, I saw my efforts as part of the larger picture of Kingdom-building that I was blessed to experience.

The first aspect of servanthood is that the person must see himself as a team player, like Drew Brees, the very popular quarterback for the New Orleans "Who Dat" Saints. He was the team's leader, but he also had to be conscious that he was a team player. His fellow team members respected him as quarterback, but they also liked him. The linebackers and receivers had to like Brees and they had to like each other, because that is the key to winning. Team players play on winning teams.

People must generally like you, because they are going to have to help you serve. The nurse's ministry of Greater St. Stephen Full Gospel Baptist Church in New Orleans included my friends; the ministry also included all of the church deacons. They knew that I had a readied willingness to be part of the leadership team of Bishop Paul S. Morton. Though I've been away for a few years on my present pastoral assignment, I can still return right now and would be welcomed, almost as if I never left.

Secondly, there really can be no hidden agendas or selfish ambitions for greatness when you're called to serve. It is not that there are not opportunities to have those kinds of pretentious and all-encompassing ideas of your own or have them suggested or encouraged by well-meaning others. The problem is that this kind of thinking is not characteristic of servanthood.

When you have a servant's attitude, you do not serve in order to gain something for yourself, outside of the one you serve; nor do you serve in order to get somewhere that would provide some measure of personal recognition or positional upgrade.

It was inevitable that in my servant position, others would approach me about preaching in their ministries. They didn't know me and probably didn't know the extent of any ability that I may have had in that arena. They just knew whom I served. How many preaching engagements did I turn down over the years? How many churches, which were actively seeking pastors, did I decline acceptance before finally departing Greater St. Stephen and Bishop Morton to accept Greater Antioch?

I had to complete a season of service, of this I had no doubt. I was not going to allow vain ambition and group prodding to cause me to lose focus and gain beneficial impartation from Bishop Morton and those with whom he enabled me to have regular and rewarding contact.

The third aspect of servanthood may be described as the exhibition of humility. For anyone, humility is a virtue. It is something that is often desired and attempted, but is very difficult to acquire and even more difficult to maintain in a society and an environment that promotes popularity. Arrogant people are filled with vanity and they love to draw attention to themselves. Even if it will only result in temporary vainglory, for them, it's really worth the effort and a pseudo-position of a servant can easily push them further into their arrogance.

It is not so with a humble servant. Humility comes from a Greek word keno-doxian which means lowly-minded. It is only mentioned in the New Testament, which means only followers of Christ would understand the context of its use. Similarly, in English, there is a process called kenosis, which means to pull or take off.

Admittedly, it is not easy to explain to a person the need to step out of the spotlight or to avoid sharing the spotlight with the person that he is serving. Perhaps it makes a person feel less than competent, capable or appreciated. Yet the Bible is filled with examples of characters in Scripture who made sure that their positions decreased while their masters' positions or the positions of those they served increased.

As David prayed in the assembly, he was careful not to assert a position of shared glory with God. He had to say to himself the reality of who he was, and that even as king, he was always under God's dominion and authority.

1 Chronicles 29:11 (CEB)

To you, Lord, belong greatness and power, honor, splendor, and majesty, because everything in heaven and on earth belongs to you. Yours, Lord, is the kingship, and you are honored as head of all.

Obviously, my critics will say that's something that should be easy to do, because the example speaks to the attitude of a man (David) towards God. The truth of that cannot be denied, but neither should we deny the principle that it teaches. The point is that David laid aside his own competencies, skills, and talents, and became a servant, subjecting himself to the glory of his time with God. Likewise, Jesus made it clear that even He was not in popular competition with His Father. He only spoke what the Father said and His assignment was to do the "will of the Father."

The final aspect or attribute of servanthood is that he gives thought first to the person that he is serving. A genuine servant gladly and willingly sacrifices his own preferences and privileges for the person he is serving. Jesus went as far as to wash the feet of His disciples. His own disciples took Jesus to task for the act and resisted His efforts to demonstrate what became for them a learning moment. In fact, of the many acts that Jesus did, washing the feet of the disciples was one that confused people about Him. When He could have reveled in His own glory, He became "as a servant." This was neither an action indicating weakness nor one that suggested defiance on His part.

The worldview of servanthood differs from that which was and is extolled by Jesus. The worldview emphasizes promotion, status and authority entrusted to and part of the character of the "one at the top." It suggests positional greatness and not greatness spawned by deference to others. In other words, the greatness is in the serving, not recognition that comes by serving.

I cannot count the times that I have carried the Bibles, robes or garment bags of Bishop Morton, but I can tell you that I did not feel denigrated at any time. I'm sure there were those times when observers labeled me as a flunky, a slave, or perhaps even a fool as I went about my assigned and anointed tasks in a spirit of excellence. (My 6'7" 270 pound stature probably prevented them from saying it to my face.)

None of that mattered to me then, and it certainly doesn't matter to me now. They could not see what God had shown me, nor were they privy to the intimacy that I had with God that generated the relationship between Bishop Morton and me.

WHATEVER IT TAKES

The cupbearer in this Old Testament story was responsible for serving wine at the king's table and protecting the king. He tasted each cup of wine before it was presented to the king as a precaution against the king being poisoned by his enemies. One of his essential qualifications and attributes was that he had to be willing to die for the king.

There are numerous occupations that a person may have aspired toward, but a career as a cupbearer was often a life or death decision. Needless to say, it was unlikely there was a long list of applicants, especially if the king was unpopular. Yet, the office of the royal cupbearer was a position of great honor in the Persian court.

Being in the daily presence of the king and seeing him relaxing on his throne or lounging on his bed of splendor was a privilege that only a few in the kingdom would have. I had the acquaintance of a man who served as the head of the White House household staff for four Presidents. It is amazing to hear the stories and the accounts of the events and personalities that he experienced over 30 years in that position. He could not recall the number of kings, princes and Heads of State that he had personally served from his respected position of a contemporary cupbearer.

It is important to note that the cupbearer had many opportunities to also gain the king's favor. From the confidential nature of his duties and his frequent access to the royal presence, he was the recipient of great trust from the king. It was incumbent upon this servant to do whatever it takes in order to curry the favor of the king.

There was nothing wrong with that being a desire of the servant. I bring it up only because many who are called upon to serve have imposed upon themselves limitations and restrictions that retard their own success—success that should come naturally as a result of the position held.

To be trusted is a greater compliment to receive than to be loved.[2] I've seen this play out in my own life and the narrative supports that it is something to seriously consider as a servant. Can the person you serve trust you?

---

[2] MacDonald, George, December 10, 1824 - September 18, 1905 Scottish author and minister.

The cupbearer knew that his destiny, the destiny of his family, and, as a practical matter, the destiny of the entire country was locked inside of his leader. This is a powerful statement because the inferences and implications extend beyond run-of-the-mill relationships. When you add to that the role of an armor-bearer to a spiritual leader, you can begin to realize that whatever you are supposed to become may be locked inside your Man of God. If you, for whatever reason, allow something or someone to discourage or kill what God has placed in you, you may never become what you are supposed to be.

I was called to be what I am before I was formed in my mother's womb. You may not be called to preach, but you are called to do something. I'm here to tell you that thing will never manifest itself until you fulfill the assignment to your leader's vision.

Luke 16:1-13 is a parable that Jesus used regarding a just and an unjust steward. A steward is a person who is designated to maximize the assets or holdings of someone else. A just steward gives direction and administration to his master's resources and assets in order to reassure the master, based on the trust he has placed in the steward, that his assets are protected and that the most prudent decisions about his property have been competently and justly handled.

You cannot serve God and trust in anything more than your leader's vision – not even the absoluteness of money. You have got to make the advancement of your leader *the* most important goal.

Joseph would have never been in his own position of power if he did not interpret the person's dream to which he was assigned to serve. He was connected to the person and he helped – even when he was in prison. His wrongful confinement did not prevent his anointing from flowing in pursuit of his ultimate destiny.

It's easy to be passionate about certain things. I am passionate about servanthood. That's because I learned early in my career that God had called me to something that was special and unique.

Servanthood is not an anointing that is universally distributed. By its very nature, servants are set aside for a purpose. Servants are called to a form of ministry. There is no other name for it and it must not be taken lightly by anyone.

In the narrative about Saul's mental state as he served as King of Israel, there is an interesting aspect of his quest to come out of what appeared to be a state of depression. Described in I Samuel 16:14-23, the story declared: "the Spirit of the Lord departed from Saul, and a distressing spirit from the Lord troubled him." The reason that I cite this passage as interesting is because of the language that is used: the spirit from the Lord troubled him. The text is explicit in saying that God, who had appointed and anointed Saul to be king of Israel, was now punishing or rendering judgment against Saul by way of an alien spirit that would trouble or menace him.

The chronicles of the times tell us that Saul had lost favor with God, but he was still the leader of God's people. Though he had lost favor, he had not lost standing as king. He had been disobedient to God, so there was a price that he had to pay. The interesting element goes further than the spirit of judgment, in that men in the court of King Saul surmised that the only immediate remedy that was available to the king was the music ministry of David. The servants in the court determined that the king needed someone with a unique anointing in order to neutralize the effects of Saul's depressive state. He was an excellent harpist and his giftedness in that area was about to make room for him in the King's palace.

They knew someone that they could call upon to get the job done. This was not a usual situation or they could have handled it themselves. Neither was it a natural situation; therefore, they needed to call on someone who had supernatural capabilities. It didn't matter that David was a sheepherder by training, because they could sense that he had an anointing for servanthood. Jesse, the Bethlehemite, had several sons, but David was the only one with a unique anointing for ministry.

Because of his special capacity for ministry and for service, David became one of the armor-bearers for Saul. Whenever the sad state of depression evidenced itself in Saul, it was David, this armor-bearer, who was called upon to minister to the king.

There is a lesson in this story that is applicable to those who are called to serve in the contemporary church. It is a lesson that can be easily overlooked if we cling to the fact that Saul was on his way out anyway. The same God who had caused the stifling condition in Saul also provided a means by which David's anointing for servanthood (armor-bearer) and, ultimately, kingship, would manifest itself.

The question, therefore, must be whether David would use this period of servanthood to become that for which God had prepared him, even before his birth, despite open and hostile opposition. This is what we face as anointed servants to our spiritual leaders. There will be challenges, criticisms, and crises that must be addressed from our unique perspective or vantage point.

I was forced to frame my movement in this area in three dimensions of both thinking and activity: a) preparation, b) submission and c) completion. The link or the connection between them may not be evident at first and there should be no dismay at the quandary of how I saw my way through it. It was not easy; nor was it sudden. It was, however, very successful in establishing me for Kingdom purpose.

The first dimension, preparation, means that you can't wait until you get to church to prepare for church. It is important for today's armor-bearer to be ready for the church experience every week. That's why you can't look at this position as one that is regular and routine, but a calling to Kingdom service and all that it entails.

There is the physical readiness of preparation, but there is also the spiritual readiness, and both are vitally important to ministry. You can't spend all of the night before becoming physically unprepared for what will take place on the next day. It hurts you and your leader because the signs of lack of preparation will be there.

Talent is not enough. Having a talent is good, but it requires more than talent. Having ability is great, but availability is equally important. I soon realized in my career that I could compensate for what I lacked in talent with hard work. There were some extra things that I had to do to be fully prepared for my assignment. There were even a few times when I had to dig a little deeper in order to be where I needed to be with my leader. That's the price that you pay for walking in this kind of anointing. Rather than a price paid, it's more of an investment made. The returns are always further down the line from the current assignment.

Prioritize three areas of preparation: 1) spiritual, 2) mental and 3) physical.

Spiritually, pray before you show up. Mentally, there needs to be a personal intellectual assessment. I'm not talking about an I.Q. test or academic exam. I'm talking about seriously assessing your knowledge of the Word of God, that is to be administered by your leader, who needs to know that both of you are on the same page. Physically, you need to be ready to move with him. You are there to minister to him as he ministers to the people. It is essential that you are able to be at one with him as he is at one with the Lord.

I can tell you that there is some hard work associated with being an armor-bearer, but that is to be expected because it's all part of the assignment. In the Book of Proverbs, Solomon addressed the example of the requirement of each of these areas of preparation, especially physically:

Proverbs 6:6–13 (CEB)

Go to the ant, you lazy person; observe its ways and grow wise. The ant has no commander, officer, or ruler. Even so, it gets its food in summer; gathers its provisions at harvest. How long, lazy person, will you lie down? When will you rise from your sleep? A little sleep, a little slumber, a little folding of the arms to lie down–and poverty will come on you like a prowler, destitution like a warrior. Worthless people and guilty people go around with crooked talk. They wink their eyes, gesture with their feet, and point with their fingers.

We are supposed to work the hardest. God anoints servants, not celebrities. It may be a temptation to be the latter, but that's not the purpose of the anointing. Celebrities bring too much drama to the table. You can't get around some of the personal attitudes that can present themselves in the work, including people who want to accept all the credit for the good and quickly declare, when things go wrong, that it was the fault of someone else.

One contemporary preaching topic is favor. Preachers all over the country have developed messages based on that single word, favor. Many of these messages seem to indicate that something extraordinary is going to be passed on to people – to most people. There may be some truth in that, but there must be a limitation on the expectation for receiving favor. There is no guarantee of favor. It is not absolute. It is a possibility that has a basis. To this end, favor is manifested when preparedness meets opportunity.[3]

In addition to that, you can't be continually late. Lateness guarantees mediocre job performance and it works as a negative in consideration of promotion. Mediocrity is the enemy of greatness.

The second dimension is that of submission. I get comfort and encouragement from Romans 13:1-5 (CEB):

Every person should place themselves under the authority of the government. There isn't any authority unless it comes from God, and the authorities that are there have been put in place by God.

---

[3] Howard, Ben, When Preparedness Meets Opportunity, May 27, 2006, Dawsonville, Ga.

So anyone who opposes the authority is standing against what God has established. People who take this kind of stand will get punished. The authorities don't frighten people who are doing the right thing. Rather, they frighten people who are doing wrong. Would you rather not be afraid of authority? Do what's right, and you will receive its approval. It is God's servant given for your benefit. But if you do what's wrong, be afraid because it doesn't have weapons to enforce the law for nothing. It is God's servant put in place to carry out his punishment on those who do what is wrong. That is why it is necessary to place yourself under the government's authority, not only to avoid God's punishment but also for the sake of your conscience.

This passage from Paul's epistle to the church relates to the recognition of leaders in government by members of the church. Though there is a difference between the secular and the sacred, the issue of submission remains the same in both arenas. The bottom line of the principle of submission is that submission is NOT submission, if it's done when you want to do it. It is not submission when it is given when you feel like it. It is not submission when you understand the reasons. In fact, each of these things is a contradiction to the principle of submission. Submission is submission when you don't want to submit, don't feel like submitting, and don't understand submitting, but you do it anyway. It is submission when your only response is "Tell me what you want me to do...next!"

I can candidly say that if your opinion is not asked, don't give it to anybody. That sounds harsh, but it's also being real! Two people will never agree on everything; that's why they are two different people. I don't agree with everything that Bishop Morton does, but when I don't (which is seldom), I am the only person who knows it. That's not because I'm afraid or because I'm like a sponge, soaking up everything. It's because I know bad spreads faster than good.

I learned early that, as an armor-bearer to a great man, you get invitations from all sorts of people for all sorts of reasons. I've become wise enough not to accept all of those invitations. Sometimes, my discerning spirit will sound the alarm that prevents me from falling into uncomfortably embarrassing situations.

1 Corinthians 15:33 (CEB)

Don't be deceived, bad company corrupts good character.

There are negative, angry, bitter and frustrated people clamoring for the opportunity to draw you into their circles of friendship. Don't fall for it. Don't go to their houses, attend their picnics or celebrate their graduations. It's probably a trap. This is not paranoia; it's a warning! You have to avoid comfortable contact and accommodation with people who make it clear that their primary intent is to create confusion.

They may look righteous on the outside, but you should be able to discern their deceit. You should be able to see deeper than the familiar external. You should and must be able to recognize people who just don't and won't flow or get along with anybody. They are hateful and mean. Stay away from them!

Loyalty is the key to all promotion. [Preparation, submission, completion – we covered preparation and submission. What about completion??]

Mark those who cause DIVISION!

I WAS MADE FOR THIS

1 Samuel 16:1 (NKJV)

Now the LORD said to Samuel, "How long will you mourn for Saul,

seeing I have rejected him from reigning over Israel? Fill your horn

with oil, and go; I am sending you to Jesse the Bethlehemite.

For I have provided Myself a king among his sons.

When reading passages of scripture, it is important to examine each line for its grammatical context. None of the words in scripture are just placed there for general reading, but each word is strategically placed in order to make sure that the reader gets the principal theological intent and purpose of it being there. Many sermons have been faulty in their composition because someone missed the intent or because they missed the context. The above passage is one such example where the content, as well as the context, must be examined.

The missed context is "For I have provided..." The statement was made in the *past tense.* I'm not trying to play on words with this matter, but there is a word that must not be left unrevealed. It is so simple, yet there is a hidden inference as it relates to the text. There is the possibility of more hidden value in the text when it is put under the spotlight of being an armor-bearer. If I were to paraphrase the line, it might read: "I have picked out somebody already and it may not be who you think it is."

There are some things that God has predestined. Some people have been pre-appointed for purpose. Their destiny has been settled beforehand. Samuel was talking about somebody who was not even there yet as far as he knew. God has already done something for somebody who doesn't even know about it. He's sending something your way that is going to blow your mind.

Sometimes, it happens to the person that others would least likely consider or expect. You can know that God is preparing you for something when you start saying, "There's got be more than this." The enemy has been fighting you like he has because he knows that promotion is about to be released in your life.

The pain that you have endured has been preparation for where you are going. The difficulty you have been through has built a bigger platform for God to use in your future.

No matter what has happened to you, you're too close to let your history get in the way of your destiny.

Before God does anything for you, he lets you go through some stuff first. Because you had problems, it has clouded your view and your appreciation of how significantly blessed you are. Somebody would be glad to have the problems you've had. To you it's a problem to have been stalled in traffic; but there's someone who wishes they had a car. You may have had to stand in the line a long time, but somebody else would be glad to have some legs to stand again. Your garage ceiling may be leaking, but somebody else had to drag their groceries in from the rain because they had no garage. Most of us are more blessed than we know, and it's a tragedy if you are blessed and don't know it. The enemy can come in and take it and you will never know that it's gone. You've got to thank God for where you are no matter where you are.

God has preordained THIS moment for your miracle!

Hell (and every hater) needs to get nervous because of where God is getting ready to bring you!

God anointed David to become King. This is what it means to be a Christian – the anointing. It comes from the Hebrew word *mashah*, where we get our word *mes-she-a*, or *messiah*, which means "the anointed one." Contrary to what some may think, "Christ" is not Jesus's last name. Christ means the anointed one.

David was anointed for his assignment before he was appointed to the assignment. Anyone who had a disagreement with the assignment also had a disagreement with the anointing. This is the predicament in which King Saul found himself and it was one that would be his undoing as King of Israel. Psalms 105:15 (CEB) addresses this matter specifically:

"Don't touch my anointed ones; don't harm my prophets!"

What greater clarity is needed than to know the anointing comes with authority, protection and power? Those who walk and serve in the anointing need not be so concerned with their adversaries or detractors because there is protection, destiny and purpose by God that is always in full effect. In fact, those who seek to trouble you will have to submit to God.

History has taught me that we are sometimes anointed and sent to a person or place to serve because problems are already present. Saul had already jeopardized his standing with God, and David had been recruited to carry out God's solution to that problem.

Problems act as job security for people who go to work with the anointing on their lives. You ought to be glad there was a problem because without one, they wouldn't need you. People like working with and having fellowship with people who are problem solvers.

Did you think that because the anointing is on your life that you might get out of trouble? The anointing is on your life for trouble. God knows the situation before you get to the situation, but knows that you had what it takes to deal with the situation.

It might be interesting to note here that the assignment that David received to serve Saul was only supposed to be a part-time position, but ended up being a full-time position. God created a position for him because he was skillful. David used his gift, never suspecting that it would enlarge his territory. Your gift will always make room for you. The implication is that there may not have been room before you got there. There had been no advertising or recruiting of harpists for the King. This was not one of the prestige positions in the tiers of leadership of King Saul's palace. David was only sought after when the problem showed up and wouldn't go away.

Don't be disappointed because there is no room yet. Get your foot in the door. If you get in there and go to work, what you lack in skill or talent, you can make up for in hard work.

David was so good at his job and this is what caused Saul to recognize the need to utilize him. This is how I got my first job in full-time ministry. I was good at what I did and I did it with the intent of having service appreciated, if not personally (or profitably) recognized.

Loving that which you do well and loving the person that you serve are priority thinking points for an armor-bearer. You've got to have passion for the work, but you must also put yourself into the position to have a deep down sense of love for leadership.

All of us were in shock when Bishop Morton, having served Greater St. Stephen so long, had a breakdown. The shock-wave of compassion came across like a tsunami all over the country, and particularly upon those who knew and served him well. Those from the Full Gospel Baptist Church Fellow-ship and other reformations were quick to offer whatever help they could, but Bishop Morton knew he could trust me. That is why John is my favorite of Jesus's disciples. Peter was always ready to be the first in line for everything, and Philip was always prepared to preach. There was something dif-ferent, however, about John. Because of my observation of him in Scripture, I have concluded that there is a difference in having the ability to do and having the heart to do. My philosophy has become to work like an employee, but think like a manager.

You must have the ability to minister strength and courage to your leader. The person that you are serving should be happy to see you. You cannot become one long counseling session. They must be at ease in your presence. You must have a good attitude at all times. That's saying a lot, but this is the reality of servanthood. There's no way around it. When was the last time you encouraged your leader?

You are called upon by your position and your anointing to a higher level of dedication than your peers. You should have loyalty that goes beyond personal feelings. Permit me to seek the confirmation of the Scriptures on this matter:

Acts 20:19 (CEB)
I served the Lord with great humility and with tears... Your personal feelings should never get in the way of your calling. A good servant can handle a rebuke.

Proverbs 28:23 (CEB)
Those who correct someone will, in the end, find more favor than those with flattering tongues.

Proverbs 27:5-6 (CEB)
A public correction is better than hidden love. Trustworthy are the bruises of a friend; excessive are the kisses of an enemy.

Proverbs 29:1 (CEB)
One who stays stubborn after many corrections will be suddenly broken, beyond healing.

Since you think you just have it going on, think about this: The time of rebuke is not the time for rebuttal. The flesh or carnal tendency of all of us is always to defend our actions immediately and that can bruise a relationship with your leader.

Try to maintain good relationships with other workers. This will require having a keen sense of what to do or say. When I initially became first assistant, I could do what my predecessor could. If all I could do was what he did, he could have remained in the position. It was incumbent upon me to become irreplaceable in my own servanthood.

•What makes you stand out?

•What makes you valuable?

•What is the unique gifting that you bring to the ministry?

GATHER ME 70

Numbers 11:16–17 (CEB)

The LORD said to Moses, "Gather before me seventy men from Israel's elders, whom you know as elders and officers of the people. Take them to the meeting tent, and let them stand there with you. Then I'll descend and speak with you there. I'll take some of the spirit that is on you and place it on them. Then they will carry the burden of the people with you so that you won't bear it alone.

There has been one word I have been hearing in my spirit lately. I can't explain why the lingering is there, but I know that it has caused me to give pause to this text from the Book of Numbers. The word is TRANSITION. Everywhere I turn, I keep hearing this same word—TRANSITION. When I turn on the television or listen to the radio, there is some commentary about TRANSITION.

There is something we all must understand about life. It has a way of taking us through transitions. It suggests changes, and changes come in so many forms. Changes have turning points that can impact the substance of your life, as well as the essence of your anointing.

Transition is not usually sudden. In fact, in many ways it can be subtle and the manifestation of it may not be evident immediately. Yet you can almost feel transition before it even happens.

Many of us are at a turning point, a transition of seasons, in our lives. One of the ways that you can know the seasons are changing in the natural is to observe the leaves on the trees as they begin to change colors. The trees do not change the season, but the leaves changing colors indicates that the seasons are going through a change. When people go from acting funny around you to acting grand and new, that may be a clear indication of change. You may have to deal with that or, at the very least, accommodate it. People are not able to change your season; you have changed. Stuff that used to be entertaining to you is not as funny anymore. People that you use to hang with now work on your nerves. Things that you used to love to do tend to sicken you. People you used to call all of the time may not get a call or an answer from you. I can't count the times I've had people try to intimidate me by saying that I had changed. Neither can I count the times that I responded that I had not changed. The devil is a liar; I have changed! I don't know about you, but when I go through my transitions, there is uneasiness. I can sense that something is about to change.

The only problem with the change of personal seasons is that you can miss it and not even know you missed it. Before you know it, you can be on the outside looking in – wondering, "What happened?" Take my word for it: you can't afford to miss it! God wants to use you, even though you have issues.

In this text, the children of Israel were in transition. They were the equivalent of 90 days from the Promised Land, and Moses, their leader, had determined that he was going to quit. This was not a statement rendered by Aaron, the assistant, or one of the elders in the tribes; this was Moses, God's shepherd and the leader of God's People.

It is obvious that Moses had become frustrated, discouraged, despondent, and tired. All of the conditions were there for him to conclude that it was time for him to quit. Any student of this story would be as moved as I was to explore what had driven Moses to this point. Why was it that, after all this time and getting so close, Moses felt like quitting? The problem with Moses, as it often is with any of us in leadership and service, was that he was burnt out. The struggle of him leading the people of God had become so burdensome to him that he was ready to quit.

The magnitude of his mental and spiritual depression can be easily seen in the following verse: Numbers 11:14 (CEB) I can't bear this people on my own. They're too heavy for me.

I couldn't help but focus on his saying that it was too heavy. Isn't it amazing that the closer you get to walking in what God wants you to walk in, the more difficult life seems to become?

"...Too heavy for me."

I recognize the words, as you may, as being the same words that Jesus spoke while He knelt and prayed in the Garden of Gethsemane. When He began to realize the pain and agony of the cross and that He would be under the pressure of everybody's load, the Bible says that Jesus began to be sorrowful and very heavy.

Moses cried out to God that it was getting too heavy, severe and difficult for him to bear it any longer. It revealed his state of mind. He agonized and was almost overwhelmed by a sense of the responsibilities of his office. This is one of the objectives of the devil. He desires that you become so frustrated with where you are that you cease celebrating God.

Moses was being crushed by the weight of life. It was not the number of the people that frustrated him. It was the nature of the people. It was not a matter of how many; it was about their attitudes.

There are some people you just can't please, and the children of Israel, in that season of change in history, were in that category.

Numbers 11:4-6 (CEB)

The riffraff among them had a strong craving. Even the Israelites cried again and said, "Who will give us meat to eat? We remember the fish we ate in Egypt for free, the cucumbers, the melons, the leeks, the onions, and the garlic. Now our lives are wasting away. There is nothing but manna in front of us."

They were close to the Promised Land, yet they adamantly complained about how good things used to be in Egypt, from which they had been rescued, restored and delivered. Actually, I wish I had been there. I wish I could have been in the crowd to give a second opinion. Did they forget so quickly how their fathers were in bondage in Egypt? Did they forget or choose to ignore that they had a history of being slaves in Egypt? Had something happened that caused them to see themselves in the past, only to ignore the future that God had put in place for them?

Any sane and rational person can tell you that you cannot successfully drive forward looking in the rear-view mirror. That's why you need to detach yourself from people who are bent on bringing up your past. They are so busy talking about what you used to be and what you used to do, that they are unable to see what God is doing in your life right now. Some people will never let you grow. They neither want nor choose to see you move forward.

I'm sure there were some ringleaders who took it upon themselves to get all of the complainers together. It is amazing how quickly grumbling and complaining can spread.

Complaining leads to having a critical spirit.

Constant criticism morphs into murmuring, which is the sin of rehearsing a complaint.

Murmuring, left unchecked will breed rebellion. We can murmur about a thing for too long. We must resist and take authority over it or we will never receive what we want from God and thus begin to operate in rebellion.

Psalm 68 says,

"The rebellious dwell in a dry land."

We can miss the blessings of the Lord because we become rebellious. Rebellion is open resistance to appointed authority. It is the refusal to obey God's given leadership, whether it is outward or in the heart. If you have it in your heart, it is just a matter of time.

Moses knew that the people could not go to the next level because there was a spirit of complaining among the leadership. They made sure that Moses heard the complaints and not the compliments. It was as if nothing he had done was right. There was nothing flattering or commendable in what they said of him. You don't need anyone to flatter you and then get with other people to demean and denounce you and your efforts. Never be so naive that you fail to realize and recognize that you've allowed some people to remain around you that are not really with you.

Moses had a complaint too. The difference was that the people poured their complaints on Moses; Moses took his complaint to God.

Every good leader feels the burdens of the people they lead. Moses said it in this story, but there were countless others. Elijah expressed it and so did Jesus. Even Paul got into that mode when he expressed in 2 Corinthians 11:28-29 (The Message):

Beside everything else that I deal with, I am pressured day in and day out concerned about all the people in the church. At this point, Moses became intense and desperate, asking God to either help him or take him. He felt that he would die right there, from the intense pressure that he was feeling.

Look at God's answer:

Numbers 11:16-17 (CEB)

The LORD said to Moses, "Gather before me seventy men from Israel's elders, whom you know as elders and officers of the people. Take them to the meeting tent, and let them stand there with you. Then I'll descend and speak with you there. I'll take some of the spirit that is on you and place it on them. Then they will carry the burden of the people with you so that you won't bear it alone.

The message that I am commended to give to you is not addressed to the masses who might read this book. It's addressed to the 70. It is addressed to those who are real. Moses called out 70 leaders from a crowd of thousands. They didn't even know why they were there or selected for service. Have you ever wondered how you got selected to serve? Have you ever speculated about what would have happened had you not been in a certain place at a certain time? Have you ever marveled about how your name was called when there were others who were more qualified to hold certain positions, but were not selected?

Those 70 were being set up for a blessing. They were getting ready to take the burden. That kind of burden reallocation is necessary and proper for all who genuinely serve, because with every burden that is removed from you, God releases a blessing for them. The anointing that was on their leader was about to be transferred to them.

There is going to be some evidence when you are about to be elevated by God. First, he was anointed with oil. This is important to know because this was his prayer – to surround himself with people who had the potential to wear the same spirit.

It's probably important at this juncture for me to re-emphasize your perspective. You should view this ministry as a personal assignment, because that's what it is. It is not a platform for arrogance. I know that sounds harsh and perhaps judgmental, but this represents a fault or flaw that can consume those who fail to view serving their leaders from a spiritual standpoint. Moses typified a leader with the right perspective. He was a humble man. He wasn't arrogant. He spoke to people. He wasn't grandiose in his demeanor. He didn't talk to people as if they were his children.

The higher God takes you, the more humble you ought to become. Whenever God decides to elevate or promote, it is never based on your needs. I emphasize that it is not and never has been about you. It's based on the Kingdom's needs. It was not all of this up today and down tomorrow stuff. He knew that it wasn't about him.

Over the years, I have noted what I call the Three E's of a Level Ministry. These are personal attributes or traits that contribute to successful ministry leadership and servanthood. When the coat is passed, it would be extremely helpful to recognize these benchmarks of successful ministry as they appear. Perhaps they can be of value to you as you prepare for greater works.

1. ENERGY is the first attribute. It equates to having a passion for what you do. Passion cannot be taught. Some people just have it and it serves them well. When you have a passion, you won't get offended so easily and want to quit because someone hurt your feelings.

If you quit:

• For whom were you singing in the beginning?
• Who did you say called you in the first place?

When the enemy comes against you and tries to get you to move out of your place, tell the devil that this is your assignment and that you will be like a tree planted by the rivers of water, that shall not be moved.

You must view your ministry as labor and not just a label. I am sure that Moses picked loyal men and women who were already in their places. He did not have to look for them. They were not people that came to work or to lead when they got ready. They were not people who were looking to receive a title. It is dangerous to give a title to someone that is lazy in the behaviors that matter.

"Civilization is always in danger when those who have never learned to obey are given the right to command."[4]

Every time Jesus picked a disciple, they were already working. God wants people who will say, "I am not sure that I am able, but I'm willing; I need your power, I need your strength, I need your anointing." God wants people who do not operate only in the flesh.

2. EMPOWER is the second attribute. A leader will have the anointing to empower others.

Some have described it as an infectious enthusiasm. It is exampled by the ability to encourage others to do more, rather than discouraging others to do less. Obviously, it requires a level of personal commitment. You can't expect people to follow you, if you can't follow another. The ministry of Moses was clearly born out of misery. Power is the sum total of all the painful experiences that you have had. When God elevates you, what you did at entry level won't work on the management level.

I used to be a good basketball player in high school. I was All Everything in athletics. No one could stop me. I received a few scholarship offers from several colleges and universities, but I turned them down because I wanted to attend and play at LSU. I genuinely believed that those little schools weren't on my level.

---

[4] **Bishop Fulton J. Sheen**

I didn't get a scholarship at LSU, so I became a walk on. I had seen them on television and I knew I could hang. On the first day of practice, we played a scrimmage to see who would practice with the varsity team. I killed them! Dunking and running the point at 6'4", I passed the 1st level.

I did get to practice with the varsity and I realized early on that they were bigger. Even so, I believed I could play. I waited my turn and when I got in the game, they destroyed me! I was so embarrassed.

After practice, one of the older coaches, Tex Winter, pulled me to the side and said, "Son, you are a good player." I was sort of surprised at that compliment on my playing since I was convinced that it was the worst showing I had ever put on in my playing history. So, I asked the disturbing question: "Why did I do so badly?" His response was, "Because you had been used to playing with B Level players. In order for you to survive this TRANSITION, you are going to have to hang around some A-Level Players."

I can say the same thing to you: if you are going to move to the next dimension, you are going to have to hang around some A Level layers. They work harder and don't complain about it. In A Level ministries, the people flow with the vision; they attend all of the services; they tithe, give, and sow seeds.

Yet, new levels bring on new devils. Old prayers won't work. The higher you go, the more the devil attacks. Some of you are under attack, not for where you are, but for where you are going.

I am thoroughly convinced in my spirit that to be an armor-bearer is one thing, but it's a whole lot different than being a pallbearer. I've seen situations where the leader appeared drained because of the insufficiency of the armor-bearer. The people who I have around me and who really are concerned about me try not to tell me too much. This one is not getting along with that one or saying this about the other one. They keep it from me, because they know it's in my DNA to try and fix it. I'll call people and handle the problem. I'll stay up all night trying to figure out a plan.

Be careful how you carry yourself and how much interest you show in the work because the 70 will have your spirit.

3. The final E is for EXECUTION. It is so interesting when people have much to say, but put so little of it into practice or action. I want to be surrounded by people who hate to lose and who have the attitude that if they are involved in a ministry, neither they nor that ministry will not fail. I want people around me who get the job done.

Numbers 11:25 (CEB)

The LORD descended in a cloud, spoke to him, and took some of the spirit that was on him and placed it on the seventy elders. When the spirit rested on them, they prophesied, but only this once.

Great ministry is not just the result of the anointing on my life. The result of great ministry is the anointing on the lives of those surrounding me. These are the people on whom I can place my coat. Elijah essentially told Elisha, "If you see me when I am caught up, if you continue to walk with me, and if I can count on you when I go through all of this craziness in the Kingdom, you can have a double portion of what God has given to me."

I am not trying to nor have I ever tried to be a superstar, but I've got this anointing on me to execute support to my leader's vision. History bears out that these 70 were among the leaders, who after the death of Aaron, defeated King Arad, the Canaanite, at a place called Hormah. This name means Utter Destruction. That's what God is going to do for you – utterly destroy every demon that's been trying to kill you.

You must begin to realize that what used to work at entry level does not work at management level. The harder you bounce the ball, the faster it comes back to you.

I'M PUSHING TO MY DESTINY

Nehemiah 2:17–20 (CEB)

So I said to them, "You see the trouble that we're in: Jerusalem is in ruins, and its gates are destroyed by fire! Come, let's rebuild the wall of Jerusalem so that we won't continue to be in disgrace. "I told them that my God had taken care of me, and also told them what the king had said to me. "Let's start rebuilding!" they said, and they eagerly began the work.

But when Sanballat the Horonite, Tobiah the Ammonite official, and Geshem the Arab heard about it, they mocked and made fun of us. "What are you doing?" they asked. "Are you rebelling against the king?"

"The God of heaven will give us success!" I replied. "As God's servants, we will start building. But you will have no share, right, or claim in Jerusalem."

he Book of Nehemiah spells out God's plan for rebuilding for us. The entire book provides principles and insights that address the issues of rebuilding. Whether you are talking about rebuilding a life, a church, a business, a community, or a city, the Book of Nehemiah gives a blue print of exactly what you need to do in order to be successful. It also addresses how to handle your co-workers as well as how to handle people whose aim it is to stifle what is to be done.

Permit me to address this topic by reviewing a few specific chapters, because I think it is important that we examine the approach that was employed by those in leadership to focus on what God had promised, as opposed to becoming bogged down in what the enemy would introduce to stifle their initiative.

In Chapter 1 God, through Nehemiah, gave the mindset that we should have in order to rebuild our lives. It is not going to be who we thought it would be to help us to rebuild. It is only going to be a remnant. You are going to need people in your life who are concerned about you and not merely concerned what you can do for them.

A close examination of the text clearly indicates that the people were in a state of malaise, where it appeared that they had lost the respect of the people around them. Their willingness to rebuild did not match their desire to work. Times can come where negativity and discouragement can completely consume groups of people. It can be a formidable weapon of the enemy and you have to be sensitive enough and have spiritual discernment enough to recognize its manifestations. It was time for a leader to rise up and assume his post and allow God's plan for the restoration of the walls to go forward.

Because the walls had been knocked down, their defenses were knocked down. They had to develop another level of consciousness of God and become particularly watchful about who they were allowing to speak into their lives.

As another consideration, if we are going to rebuild, we must confess that at some point we have messed up. We must be willing to change because it is a waste of time to rebuild with the same stuff that did not work before.

In Chapter 2, the focus was on motivation. After hearing that the walls were broken down, Nehemiah went back to work, serving King Artaxerxes in the palace. The King noticed that Nehemiah was not himself. He didn't have to say anything in order to detect a change in his demeanor. The King was sensitive to him. It's a wonderful thing to have people in your life who are not so caught up in themselves that they become insensitive to what is going on in the life of someone else with whom they have daily contact.

God is going to surround you with some people who can really help you, as well as those who you want to help you. A real friend will always send you to praise and will never pull you away from praise. You've got to make up your mind that if you are going to rebuild your life, it has to begin with praise. Just like the workers in the story, there has to be a praise priority put in place.

There are, then, at least four areas of focus when you undertake the task of rebuilding your life for service to the Kingdom. **The first is DEVOTION.** There has to be some time set aside for personal devotion. This is time that you spend inviting the Holy Spirit to endow you with a sense of urgency in accepting where God is leading you and what He is already doing in your life.

The second area of focus is that of DISTRACTION. It happens all the time and is among the most subtle of Satan's tools. His desire has always been to deceive the believer; when that believer is also a leader or anointed to serve leadership, greater intensity is placed on this effort.

As soon as the leader had engaged in his personal devotion, the second area set in. Sanballat came against him. If you are going to rebuild your life, you are going to have to develop the skill to handle critical people. Moses had to stand in the face of Pharaoh himself and say what God said – not what his body said and not what his bills said.

Nehemiah had not even started on the project before his critics came after him. The enemy doesn't want you to start. He wants you to procrastinate. In fact, he dares you to start because he knows that starting is the seed to finishing.

"You can't go to the dealership. Your credit is too bad."

"Don't try to start that new business. Don't you know how many people tried and failed?

"Do you dare sow that seed? Do you know what your bills look like?"

You can avoid the consequences of Satan's distractions. It just depends upon how badly you want a breakthrough. Though distraction was in his face, Nehemiah continued on his assignment.

The third area is DISCIPLINE. It is defined as a heartfelt promise to yourself from which you will not back down. Most failures in life are not the result of the lack of ability. They come from a lack of discipline. In Christianity, we do a great job teaching on love, but we often fail in teaching and preaching on discipline. Consequently, we live in a world of lack...

Lack of health.
Lack of wealth.
Lack of rest.

You've got to be disciplined enough to realize that even though your work may appear to go unnoticed and others keep getting the promotions, there will come the time, a time already ordained by God, that you will not be passed over. The time will come when you will go to the head of the line. In fact, you may be next in line, but without discipline, the reward of promotion may be delayed in coming to you.

It is sometimes difficult to convince those with whom you work that there is a special anointing for purpose on your life. Inevitably, perhaps because of our egos, we sense the need to get validation of what God has told us from others. This amounts to getting other folks to affirm what God said only to you. I bring it up because in this text, Nehemiah did not immediately tell anyone what God had said. He even employed some secretive movements in order to prepare for what God and the King had promised him. He purposefully told no one initially what he was doing. I can both understand and appreciate Nehemiah's position, because there have been times when I couldn't tell anyone what God had placed on my heart. What good would it have done? It wouldn't have enhanced what He had promised. Would it have been only to establish in someone's mind that I had a talk with Him?

This is what I do know: Never tell people who can't help you get there where you are going.

DETERMINATION is the fourth and final attribute. One of the things that gives me hope in difficult times is the security in knowing that God not only loves us, but that along with His love comes His strengthening power to sustain us. He is strong enough to take broken disconnected pieces of my life, and like a conductor in a symphony orchestra, pull it all together to sound harmonious and beautiful, and as though they were never disconnected.

Brokenness in any form can hinder you from being everything that God would have you to be. If you have ever had your heart broken, the real problem may not be in the fact that someone hurt you. It is that this brokenness can hinder you from receiving real love when it comes. If you have ever had someone to constantly belittle you to the point where it destroys your self-esteem, you can become negative and bitter towards others because of the way you feel about yourself.

When you have been through an emotionally traumatic situation and your spirit has been broken, it becomes extremely difficult to experience joy on the same level as before. If that is the case, it can be the foundation of all weakness in you.

Nehemiah had seen the broken condition of his city. He also recognized that the only people he had to help him rebuild were people who were already broken themselves. How does God expect broken people to rebuild anything, when what they need is someone else to rebuild themselves?

There was a time when I wasn't getting the support that I needed. I complained about it in places and with people who I thought could change the responses I had been receiving. Instead, those people laughed at me and the disillusionment was so great that I thought I would crumble and quit. When they said I'd never amount to anything, I'd slump into a depression or try to defend myself and my actions.

Now, after all that I've been through, I've discovered that I'm better when my back is against the wall.

We can learn more about ourselves in adversity than in victory.

In adversity, we dig deeper to find the real 'winner' in us. It's like a woman getting pregnant. She received a seed; the moment she became pregnant, her cycle stopped. Pregnancy breaks the cycle. The same parallel exists when you get real revelation. It will break cycles in your life.

God is getting ready to break somebody's cycle. I keep getting these revelations about what God has for me:

Pictures of me prosperous.
Pictures of me being happy.
Pictures of me going to the next level.

I'm still here because God is not through with me, yet. You can have a similar revelation, but you've got to get the wall up. You need to spend some time in DEVOTION. You need to press pass DISTRACTIONS. You need to DISCIPLINE your flesh and be DETERMINED that you will not quit.

There is a word in the Hebrew (Zalah) which generally expresses the idea of a successful venture. It literally means to push forward. Without my pushing forward, my life cannot and will not be rebuilt. The Bible says that after Joshua died, and the children of Israel had reached the Promised Land, another generation arose but did not know the Lord or the works that He had done for them. Like most people, they were blessed and forgot it was the Lord that brought them out; they had gotten so used to the blessing that they forgot about the Blesser. Zalah is very close to the word Halah, which is the root word to Hallelujah! When the Bible says, "Faith comes by hearing and hearing by the Word of God," even if you are the person saying it, you can develop faith for that situation. Thus, the more you say "He's pushing me," the more you will begin to understand that your life begins to line up with the words that are coming out of your mouth.

Ultimately, you are going to have victory over every test and every challenge in your life. Saying those words along with God's Enablement and God's Power, you are able to overcome any test, trial, circumstance or situation that occurs in your life.

It will enable you to live the life God has planned for you, rather than what you want to do. God's power to help you is not there to serve your agenda. He already has an agenda for your life. He will anoint you to do what He has called you to do.

The anointing of God Is His enablement to do what in and of yourself, could not be done by your strength.

When people witness your doings, it can cause them to misjudge you. When they see you do things with God's strength behind you, they may conclude that it is easier than it really is. What they did not see, however, was that quietly and behind the scenes, God was pushing you. Because you aren't falling to pieces, people may think that you are strong. They expect you to react to situations the way they would respond. That creates a problem for some of them. They won't help you or minister to you because they don't think you need anything. They have no idea that beneath all of that show of strength is a frail human being.

Have you ever surprised yourself and said, "How did I make it through that?" It was God's strength that was maintaining you. If you ever get that confused and think that is was your strength, alone, you are setting yourself up for the greatest disappointment of your life.

The Bible says something that has always terrified me: Sampson, who was a strong man, shook himself and wished not that his strength had departed. He did not recognize that his strength was gone and thought that he could always do what he had always done. He did not recognize that God had 'stepped back' for a moment in order for him to see that it was not him doing it; but it was the strength of God helping him do it.

When God adds increase in your life, you will be able to do things that you would not normally be able to do.The task was great - too great for a bunch of 'broken people'. Satan is aware of who you are and is trying to prove that the test is greater than God's strength. He is in a covenant with you. It's better to workout with somebody who is stronger than you are. Yet, Goliath fell to ground like lightening because God got behind the rock. His power pushed it through Goliath's head. Perhaps, if it were not for the push of God's Hand, the rock would have fallen off Goliath like a raindrop.

Some of you can relate to those facts. There is nothing exceptional about you. The reason you're where you are is that He can take substandard equipment and perform supernatural feats. The reality is that I made it by the push of God. If you were to remove the smooth stones from Goliaths forehead, you would notice that there was nothing 'exceptional' about that rock. Similarly, if you exhume David and were to raise him from the dead, there was nothing 'exceptional' about David's hand. All he had was a slingshot - a child's toy.

CATCH THAT COAT!

2 Kings 2:9–10 (NKJV)

"And so it was, when they had crossed over, that Elijah said to Elisha, Ask! What may I do for you, before I am taken away from you? Elisha said, Please let a double portion of your spirit be upon me. 10 So he said, you have asked a hard thing. Nevertheless, if you see me when I am taken from you, it shall be so for you, but if not, it shall not be so."

We are living in a time where everybody is talking about 'the anointing'. It has almost become a buzzword in the Body of Christ. The mere mention of the word, 'anointing' brings about a certain level of excitement and anticipation. Unfortunately, while the anointing is powerful, it is also quite often misused. Many things and people that we call anointed are not anointed at all; because the music is loud does not mean it's anointed. We are quick to conclude that the anointing is represented in places and upon people to which 'anointing' is foreign. It has become so easy for us to use the anointing as an explanation of things we don't understand and of people who appear to be different.

The anointing has change characteristics that can be in something, but it doesn't have to be the something that it is in. It's not music, but it can be in music. The anointing is not preaching, but it can be in preaching. It's not excitement, but it can cause excitement. Someone can excite us to shout, but the question is can they empower me to change. Can they encourage me to reach my destiny?

Allow me to define the anointing in language that can be understood and that has practical application.

The anointing is the manifested personality and power of God in the yielded life of a believer, for a specific task and for a specific time.

Even if you are unable to recite a theologically- based definition for 'the anointing', a believer can look at somebody and know that there is something different about them. First, the anointing cannot be based upon whether or not the person can perform. That's talent. To be anointed means to have 'the kiss of God on your life.

The anointed of the Lord can do more with less. Things that are hard for other people are easy because you are anointed to do them. When you are anointed, you can hold on when other people let go.

As a matter of fact, the anointing moves you into a dimension of God that you didn't even know you could handle.

Contrary to what people think, the anointed is not based upon what is on the outside, but what is on the inside. It is an outward sign indicative of an inward grace. When you are anointed, there is inner strength. It's not something that you can emulate or imitate.

I have found that we want the POWER of the anointing and the PRESENCE of the anointing but very few people want to pay the PRICE for this anointing. It's not cheap. It's is not free and it does not come easily.

There is, however, a PROCESS by which we can obtain this anointing. We will appreciate the power of God when we begin to understand the process required to attain it in our lives.

Two things need to be considered regarding the anointing. It is tangible. You can hear it, see it, smell the aroma, taste and touch it. That's why, when I attend church, I want to sit next to someone who is anointed. That's because the anointing is contagious. When you're sitting next to someone who is anointed, you can tell it, the same way as if you are sitting next to someone who is hateful.

The anointing is also transferable.

Your anointing comes from somewhere and more specifically from somebody. Whenever they got ready to anoint prophets, priests and kings, they never started with the hands first. They always started with the head and wherever the head is anointed, the body would be anointed as well. If I should check the 'oil on the skirt', it should have the same consistency as the head. However, if a part of the body is disconnected, that means that it will not have received this anointing.

If the leader is anointed, you can receive a 'double portion' of his anointing. This is often the desire of those who recognize the anointing upon their leader and who desire that much or more on themselves. As we see in the text, this is not an unusual request or desire. In fact, it's well within reason, provided you understand the price of the leader's anointing. How many times have you heard these acclamations and tributes to our leaders?

"Oh, my pastor is so blessed."
"My pastor is so anointed."
"My pastor is spiritually awesome!"
"My life has changed because of the anointing on his life."

All of that is commendable, but has there been any thought given that in order to get the 'double portion' of his anointing, there is also the requirement to go through everything that it took to get that anointing. Are you ready for a double the amount of pain and betrayals? Are you willing to go through what he went through to get to where he is?

We have glamorized the benefits and results of the anointing until people think that it's easy. There is a process. There is a journey.

Elisha understood it. He understood that there was a process. He served Elijah and knew that his anointing would have to come from Elijah. He knew how God had used Elijah. He had heard of how God fed him during a drought, used him to raise a boy from the dead and how God used him to destroy the 450 prophets of Baal.

Because he knew what he wanted, Elisha was willing to go through the process. If you want to have the 'double portion,' you've got to go through the process. I could go on continually about 'the process', but it might be served best by identifying some strategic stops that were made by the prophet as he became enriched in the things of God in this text from II Kings 2. It identifies four strategic locations that, for me, bear great significance in understanding 'the process'. The four places are Gilgal, Bethel, Jericho and Jordan.

1 Kings 2:1 (NKJV)

And it came to pass, when the Lord was about to take up Elijah into heaven by a whirlwind, that Elijah went with Elisha from Gilgal.

Gilgal has been considered the place where all great ministries begin. It was where the first Israelite encampment was established and the place where Joshua crossed Jordan. It was the place where Joshua made a circular altar for worship.

The original word was actually 'Gal-ga', which means roll or 'circle'. If you are going to receive the 'double portion', it will look like your life is going around in circles, on the treadmill of life, going through the motions. It's like being in motion, but going nowhere. It's like being at work, but receiving no reward for your labor.

Gilgal was the first place of worship and sacrifice. It was where blood was shed from circumcision. The second place which has meaning in this discussion is Bethel.

2 Kings 2:2 (NKJV)

Then Elijah said to Elisha, "Stay here, please, for the LORD has sent me on to Bethel." But Elisha said, "As the LORD lives, and as your soul lives, I will not leave you!" So they went down to Bethel.

It was the spiritual center of the Kingdom. It was the place where Jacob saw the angels ascending and descending, up and down the ladder. This is talking about heavenly angels but earthly angels or messengers, pastors, going up into the mind of God and, then, back down, to give the people an understanding of what God has said.

Bethel was the place of revelation. It was the place where the Ark of the Covenant, which housed the Presence of God, was kept.

'Beth' - House
'El' - God

The enemy wants you to leave Bethel. He wants you to leave your blessed place. The enemy is trying to get you to come out of the house, because he knows that if he gets you out of the house, he won't need to curse you. By coming out of the blessed place, you will curse yourself.

He is trying to reach you. He has started to dangle bait in front of you. His desire is to entice you, trying to get you to do your own thing - playing on both sides of the fence. He wants you to have your cake and eat it too.

There is also a doctrine quietly at work in the text. It's called the 'Doctrine of Balaam'. Balak had employed Balaam to perform a curse on the children of Israel. This sorcerer could not find a way to curse the children of Israel because they were blessed by God. The devil cannot curse what God has blessed.

Blessed people don't live in the fear of being cursed or of someone taking away their blessing. That someone can try to do something to stop their blessing, but it's not going to work. The devil certainly knows that you are blessed. Again, He knows that if he gets you to come out of the house, he won't need to curse you because, by coming out of the blessed place, you will curse yourself. But you have got know where your blessed place is.

You've got to stay in the house. You can't miss going to church. You've got to make up in your mind that nobody is going to separate you from your leader. This takes us to the third place of spiritual discovery: Jericho.

2 Kings 2:4 (NKJV)

Then Elijah said to him, "Elisha, stay here, please, for the LORD has sent me on to Jericho." But he said, "As the LORD lives, and as your soul lives, I will not leave you!" So they came to Jericho.

Jericho is thought by some scholars to be the oldest city in the world and was situated near one of Palestine's strongest streams. It was an oasis in a desert - a place of rich soil and constant sunshine. It was situated at the lowest part of the Jordan Valley, 740 feet below sea level.

At this time, it was not heavily populated and separated from the society. In many ways, it was a very lonely place — a place of isolation. That says something to me about spiritual anointing because if you walk in a real anointing, you are going to have to go through your personal Jericho. *You will* experience a season of isolation.

Whenever God got ready to use someone in a significant way, it was not long before that person found himself in isolation and separated from that which was popular and which lent itself to familiarity. He spoke to Elijah in the garden **alone.** He wrestled with Jacob, **alone.** He called Moses to talk to Him, **alone.** He allowed the devil to drive Jesus into the wilderness, **alone.**

The reason that many can't get what God has for them is often because they are too worried about what people have to say.

Jericho was below sea level and so will be your Jericho. There will be numerous times when you will have to *go down* to get where God is leading you. It will be a time of prayer. The enemy will always conclude that he has you when you are down; but you are stronger when you are down.

There will always be church people watching you flow with the man of God. They will marvel at the spectacle, while calling you derogatory or demeaning names. Much of that, though aimed at you, is really for the benefit of others who may admire what you do. The intent is to poison their minds against you, but more pointedly, the leader.

Romans 16:17 (NKJV)

Now I urge you, brethren, note those who cause divisions and offenses, contrary to the doctrine which you learned, and avoid them.

Elisha had followed Elijah for years, but he refused to leave until he received a double portion of his spirit. 'Portion' could mean 'mouth' or 'words'. Jesus said, *"My words are Spirit and they are life."* You catch His spirit when you hear His words.

He is God's voice to you because he gives you the words necessary to life. When I come to church, my purpose is to get life - from his mouth, to your spirit. It's like 'mouth–to-mouth resuscitation'.

The final process step is 'impartation'. There is no de-par-tation without impartation. Perhaps, that's why this fourth location, Jordan, is so important.

2 Kings 2:6 (NKJV)

Then Elijah said to him, "Stay here, please, for the LORD has sent me on to the Jordan." But he said, "As the LORD lives, and as your soul lives, I will not leave you!" So the two of them went on.

The Jordan River, is more than the place where Jesus was baptized or one more place that had to be crossed by Israel. The Jordan River was a place of pain, because many battles took place at or near The Jordan River. It was the final crossing place for the children of Israel to get to the Promised Land. They are two problems that should be noted regarding the Jordan and Israel: They didn't want to follow Moses out and they didn't want to follow Joshua in.

They had left Egypt and were on their way to the Promised Land, but were stuck in the middle of a place called, The Jordan River. It was 150 to 200 miles long, about 60 feet wide and about 5-8 feet deep. This small and seemingly insignificant river almost kept the Israelites out of the Promised Land. They were eager to enter the Promised Land; they were eager to live in peace, but first, they had to cross the waters of Jordan.

Tradition says that every time they got ready to cross, the river rose. Indeed, every time you get ready to cross over to the other side of your present circumstance, problems rise. You are supposed to experience your 'Promised Land', now, but there is a Jordan River trying to stop you.

Some people, undoubtedly, turned back. They quit prematurely and were wrong. Regardless of the issue, no situation should so overwhelm you or become depressing to you that you want to turn back or quit. In fact, that's contrary to our declaration of faith and trust in God. No sickness can overtake you. No disease can kill you. No weapon formed against you will prosper.

When they got to the other side, the Bible said they shouted. This is how you can tell if you are really ready for the 'double portion'. It is when you can look a problem in the face and shout about it.

Because Elisha went through the process, he was ready for the Double Portion. He went through Gilgal, going around in circles, to Bethel where he made his way to the House of God, passed through Jericho, finding 'a season of separation', and finally, to Jordan, where his problems began to rise.

It was only after going through all of that, did the coat of Elijah fall, and Elisha picked it up. Some of you are not just qualified, but 'overqualified'. After all the hell you've been through, you may be overqualified to get the coat.

When you have the double portion, your enemies will bow at your feet. Every demonic force has to bow at the feet of somebody who is anointed.

Sickness, poverty, lying spirits and other demons are going to tremble when they see you coming.

Catch your leader's spirit.

A double portion is an inheritance for the 'loyal follower'.

2 Kings 2:11-12 (CEB)

They were walking along, talking, when suddenly a fiery chariot and fiery horses appeared and separated the two of them. Then Elijah went to heaven in a windstorm. Elisha was watching, and he cried out, "Oh, my father, my father! Israel's chariots and its riders!" When he could no longer see him, Elisha took hold of his clothes and ripped them in two.

Notice he said "my father, my father" and not "my friend, my friend." I have come to recognize that one of the greatest hindrances to the power of God moving in our churches is something called a 'familiar spirit.' A familiar spirit can manifest in several different ways. But the one that applies here is that we can become so familiar with the person that we miss the power in their lives.

Perception determines reception.

How you perceive your leader is how you receive from them. If you only perceive them as a friend then that will be the level of anointing that is going to be released. But for where you are going you don't need a "friend's anointing." One of the reasons some of us are in the trouble we are in now is because of our friends. The next level or double portion anointing is going to be released when we see our leaders at another level.

While I believe it is very important for leaders to be friendly, I believe it's dangerous when we look at them at the same level as our friends. There has to be a different level of respect.

1 Timothy 5:17 (NIV)

The elders who direct the affairs of the church well are worthy of double honor, especially those whose work is preaching and teaching.

2 Kings 2:13 (CEB)

Then Elisha picked up the coat that had fallen from Elijah. He went back and stood beside the banks of the Jordan River.

Because he was in his place when Elijah dropped his coat he was able to get it. Because he was in his place when the anointing fell.

You never can tell when the coat is going to fall. That's why it is important to be in your place at all times. When I was working with Bishop Morton, we had seven worship experiences – every Sunday! And I went to every one, every Sunday, even before I was on full-time staff. When the coat fell, I wanted to be in place to get it. I'd realized that loyalty is the key to all promotion.

2 Kings 2:14 (CEB)

He took the coat that had fallen from Elijah and hit the water. He said, "Where is the Lord, Elijah's God?" And when he hit the water, it divided in two! Then Elisha crossed over.

You will cross over into your destiny, sense the certainty of purpose, and have dreams fulfilled when you 'catch the coat.'

2 Kings 2:15 (CEB)

The group of prophets from Jericho saw him from a distance. They said, "Elijah's spirit has settled on Elisha!" So they came out to meet him, bowing down before him.

Elisha is now wearing Elijah's coat. And the same enemies that tried to attack him recognized that he now is wearing Elijah's coat. There should be something about you that reminds people of the person you serve. If they are kind, you should be kind too; if they are punctual you should be punctual also. If you are a minister you should have some recognizable traits of the person that you have been listening to. If not, it will be more challenging for *your* listeners, who know your leader, to receive from you.

Elisha received a double portion. So much so that Elijah had 32 miracles and Elisha and 64. That's twice as many! But what you must understand is that Elisha had a servant by the name of Gehazi. And by simple math Gehazi should have had a double portion of Elisha's spirit. But he missed his opportunity because he was not in the right place at the right time. He didn't have the right spirit, disposition and attitude.

Let's follow the example of Elijah so that when the coat drops, you'll be in place to CATCH THAT COAT!

WHATEVER HE GAVE YOU... WORK IT!

Matthew 25: 14–15 (NKJV)

For the kingdom of heaven is like a man traveling to a far country,
who called his own servants and delivered his goods to them.
And to one he gave five talents, to another two, and to another one,
to each according to his own ability; and immediately
he went on a journey.

In Matthew 25, we have the occasion of Jesus giving one of the building blocks of life. It was a set of conditional principles for living a bountiful, successful and worthwhile life. It was also a lesson on the inherent personal responsibility of being accountable. It was very simple and certain: If you will do this, a certain result will occur; if you do something other than that, this will happen.

This teaching method actually begins in Matthew 20, in his discussion of 'the Kingdom of heaven', where He gave a series of comparisons, using what came to be known among students of Scripture as parables. 'It's not this, but it's like this'. I could go into a grammatical or contextual explanation of a 'parable', but for the sake of getting to the point of this chapter, permit me to define it this way: A parable is when you compare something that you *can* understand to explain something that you would *never* understand.

Jesus used the terminology of that day to explain pro-found Biblical Truths, because in order to be effective in preaching and servant leadership, you have to reduce it to the lowest common denominator. Jesus was giving them some of the "How To's" of life.

This particular parable was used to teach about talents. When you look at the talents, you have to first look at them literally. A talent was money; more specifically, it was the equivalent of 200 lbs. of gold. Since today's value of gold is about $900 an ounce; that's about $3 million. So, with these three men, we can roughly estimate that one was given 5 talents or $15 million; another was given 2 talents or $6 million; and the other was given 1 talent or $3 million. These were significant amounts of money and represented a great deal of trust and confidence by all involved.

We should not only view the talents literally, but we also have to apply the talents metaphorically. In that sense, a talent can also be an innate gift, which all of us possess. All of us have at least one a gift - one talent that God gave to us upon conception. One of the reasons that we are subject to personal and spiritual attack is because we are uniquely gifted. No one attacks the person on the corner, holding a sign saying, 'I'll work for food'. The enemy never attacks you for yesterday's problems. He attacks you because of tomorrow's promises.

A talent may also be defined as an opportunity, because you can be given an opportunity that is a five-talent opportunity, a two-talent opportunity or a one-talent opportunity. Jesus described the Kingdom of Heaven as being like a man, who gives his workers a tremendous amount of revenue, gifting or opportunity, expecting each one to recognize it, work it and multiply it. He also expects each to bring it back for the building of the Kingdom.

Of the three men given talents, two of them multiplied what they had. The other man buried his talent. He did not work his gift. Even if you only have one talent, that's all it takes to propel you to the next dimension of your life.

Proverbs 18:16 (NKJV)

A man's gift makes room for him And brings him before great men.

I always want to be around people that are growing — people who want to get to the next level. If you are with people who are going nowhere, they will hate you simply because of who you are. When Joseph told his brothers what God was about to do in his life, the Bible records that they 'hated him'. These were his own brothers, yet they hated him because he had favor on him. You can't help the fact that you've got favor on you. You can't help it because you're positive and they only see negativity. You can't be responsible for the fact that people like you and hate them. Most of them are not hated without reason; they are hated because they are mean.

One gift can do great things for you. There is no need to become envious of what appears to be multiple gifts in others. A singular gift can make a difference and manifest your anointing for purpose.

There are four ways to promote, grow or develop your gift. The first is serving. If you want to learn from someone, serve them. Submission is not submission, when you want to do it.

In the movie American Gangster,[5] Denzel Washington, who played the main character, Frank Lucas, got the job because he served as Bumpy's driver. Submission releases the double portion into your life. Everywhere Elijah went, Elisha went as well.

---

[5] **American Gangster, Ridley Scott, November, 2007.**

Simulation is another way to grow. Find someone who is achieving the results that you want and model their behavior. There's nothing new under the sun. Everything in one form or the other has already been done. Simulation turns decades into days.

Sowing is perhaps, the most challenging, but it is also the most rewarding for that same reason.

Matthew 10:41 (NKJV)

He who receives a prophet in the name of a prophet shall receive a prophet's reward. And he who receives a righteous man in the name of a righteous man shall receive a righteous man's reward.

If you give a righteous man a gift, you will receive a righteous man's reward. What is a righteous man's reward? The answer may be found in this Scripture:

James 5:16

...the effective, fervent prayer of a righteous man avails much (or gets God's stamp of approval).

The reward of a righteous man is answered in prayer. So, if you are in a season where you need prayers answered, find a righteous man - a just man - and put a gift at his feet. When you put that gift there, you will have set yourself up to walk in a season of answered prayer.

Matthew 10:41 (NKJV)

He who receives a prophet in the name of a prophet shall receive a prophet's reward. And he who receives a righteous man in the name of a righteous man shall receive a righteous man's reward.

You will receive what? What is a prophet's reward? It is the fulfillment of prophesies. If you have prophesies that have not been fulfilled, find a prophet and put a gift in his hand. I have lived and experienced long enough to put myself into position to walk in that level of grace.

If you are lacking in a certain area in your life, find someone who is walking in that area, and put a gift in his hand. You will walk in that same level for that season.

Fruitfulness is the evidence of God's approval or God's endorsement. When He is looking for someone to use, He is looking for someone that will be fruitful or that will multiply what he has. It is not necessarily the person who has been endowed with the most gifts, or who has the most talents; it is the person who will be most fruitful. The question is whether you can produce fruit.

All of the men were given gifts. Two of them multiplied their gifts. One of them was not fruitful and buried his gift. When this slothful servant got his talent, he put it back into himself, while the others invested their talent and multiplied to build the Kingdom.

Though you have gifts and/or talents, are you using it just for you, or are you using it to build the kingdom? I know you are a great teacher, but if you used it to build the Kingdom, God will multiply that gift and put you before great men. Before you know it, you'll get a better teaching job. Are you using it to build the Kingdom of God?

If you did, God will multiply it and put you before great men. You'll find yourself getting better contracts.

WORK WHAT HE GAVE YOU

People complain about the very thing they are supposed to be using to build the Kingdom. Secondly, he took the talent and invested it in himself. It is also a symbol of someone getting one talent. You got 100% of that one talent, and you invested all in yourself. You got the seed and spent it all on you.

Therefore, the seed had no chance to grow because you invested it all on you. You kept it all in your hand and that's all it ever became. You should take at least 10% of it and put it in God's Hand. Let Him multiply it; but he gave no effort! It seems to me that the person who had one talent should have been working harder.

Because when one's not naturally gifted, he should give a 5-talent effort, but he only gave a one-talent effort. Too many people are giving a 'one-talent effort'.

WORK WHAT HE GAVE YOU

We often seek so much from God, but we don't know how to bring Him what we already have. Every now and then, we ought to bring the LORD the little things. Quit making excuses. Just work what He gave you. When you work it, He'll give you a reason to give Him praise.

WORK IT!

God takes the little money, talent and skills and magnifies them. It all depends upon who's working it.

A baseball bat in my hands is worth $129, but a baseball bat in Derek Jeter's hands is worth $25 million. It all depends upon who's working it!

A football in my hand is worth $100, but a football in Peyton Manning's hands is worth $36 million. It all depends upon who's working it!

A basketball in my hands is worth $75, but a basketball in Lebron James' hands is worth $100 million. It all depends upon who's working it!

A tennis racket in my hands is a lethal weapon, but a tennis racket in the hands of Venus or Serena Williams is another Wimbledon title. It all depends upon who's working it!

A good microphone in my hands is worth $3,500, but a microphone in Oprah's hands is worth $1.3 billion. It all depends upon who's working it!

A computer in my hands is worth $2,000, but a computer in Bill Gates' hands is worth $50 billion. Again, it all depends upon who's working it.

Proverbs 18:16 (NKJV)

A man's gift makes room for him and brings him before great men.

The Hebrew word, 'mattan', means 'present' or 'reward'. Here, it means both, including money.

'Gift', as defined by Webster, is something you can receive with little or no effort. In a spiritual sense, it is critical that you find and exercise your gift. The evidence is clear that in doing so, it will make room for you, broaden you, make you larger and make you more open. This will also, put you before great men.

First Corinthians 12 refers to the gifts of the Spirit, given to us by the Father. These are innate gifts, given to us at birth, by the Father. All of us possess at least one of these gifts. It is part of your spiritual DNA and describes your spiritual identity.

These are also called 'motivational gifts'. What motivates you to do what you do?

Romans 12:4 (NKJV)

"4 For as we have many members in one body, but all the members do not have the same function."

God has made the body into one big puzzle and all of us are pieces, but with different functions. The pinky on my hand is small, but without it, I would be limited in what my body can do. Each person has one gift that is prominent within and sometimes he has to diligently search to find it, even in its prominence. Once you discover who you are, you will become compelled from within to walk in a very different level of peace.

The first area is the gift of prophecy, which is the eye of the body. It is the seer. This gift must be coupled with your secondary gift, ministry. They operate in conjunction and are side-by-side in terms of function and effectiveness.

In actuality, we can call it 'service'. An armor-bearer is a servant. It is a biblical position. Moses had Joshua. Saul had David, who had Jonathan. Elijah had Elisha and Paul had Timothy. Each of these characters of Scripture understood their gifting – some early, some later, some by teaching and others by impartation – and flowed in it.

Romans 1:1 (NKJV)

Paul, a bondservant of Jesus Christ, called to be an apostle, separated to the gospel of God.

Paul, using language that might be contemporarily considered denigrating, referred to himself as a bondservant or slave to the gospel. I was willing to be a slave. An armor-bearer is a servant and a gift from God.

None of us have any or all of these without measure. Don't think that because you don't have all of the characteristics of a particular gift, that you don't possess that gift. The manifestation of it may be more evident to others than to you. You can count on the fact that if you are not in your area or operating in your gift, you will be frustrated, and so will everybody around you.

Perhaps, one of the greatest challenges, as it relates to giftedness, is staying in your area. I guess it's a lot like driving an automobile. Everything works well until you start arbitrarily, capriciously or randomly changing lanes. Where the prophet or the perceiver represents the eyes of the body, no one else needs to try to lay claim to that function. You may be impressed by the level of their performance, but you have to avoid emulation due to admiration. Similarly, the teacher is the mind of the body. The exhorter is the mouth of the body.

Givers are the arms of the body. Rulers are the shoulders of the body. The 'gift of mercy' or compassion is the heart of the body.

The servers are the hands of the body. These are people who have a passion for being helpful, anytime. They love helping and being around people. They are sharp with details because they want to make it happen for the persons they are serving. No one needs to call them to do it. They just flow in this area.

Certain people have the natural gift to just find themselves working. They are very alert to practical needs and their greatest satisfaction comes from seeing a need met through their efforts.

In other words, there are certain people, who have a supernatural gift to be genuinely interested in the welfare of another person. They are more devoted to the interest of other people than they are for themselves. They don't do what they do for any other reason than to please the one they serve.

A parasite wants what's in your hand; a protégé wants what's in your heart. It's not serving to get close to the big names. I didn't serve Bishop Paul S. Morton for all those years so that I might get a church. Neither did I serve him for a check. I served because I was gifted to do it.

But I need to make it emphatically clear that I didn't quit serving when I started getting paid. I realized that my service had to go to another level.

Servants love working in the background. They don't mind working with the kids and cutting out construction paper. They could just as easily assist in a Sunday School class and not insist on being the Sunday School teacher. It might be necessary and more expedient to make somebody else look good, even if you don't shine in the best light.

Now, a person who tries to fake in this area will try to act as if they prefer being in the background, but they want to be seen. If you give them enough time, they will be exposed. You cannot be a true servant if you quietly love the limelight. Do what you have to do and move. Real servants get uncomfortable when their names are called. A fake servant loves to hear their names called. "When they are calling, are they going to call my name?"

Real servants don't try to volunteer themselves for leadership or to do self-promotion. "When is it going to be my turn?" never comes out of the mouth of a servant. There is the absence of any sense of entitlement. When they are given something to do, they go beyond what is required of them. They never say, "That is not my area!" They do anything you ask them to do.

The inevitable name-calling will occur when servant leadership is genuinely exercised and you have to be careful not to be so offended that it will affect who you are and what you are called to do. You can't be scared to be called a 'flunky'. This is different from 'worldly leadership', which demands that you claw your way to the top, by pulling other people down and walking over them.

Jesus made it clear to the disciples who walked with and followed him that if they wanted to be great, they had to learn how to serve. Regardless of what people say and the personal persecutions and abuses that you will probably have to encounter, your commitment must always be to serve.

People who are gifted to serve tend to ignore their own needs and over-extend personal energy and strength. They have difficulty in saying 'No'. At the same time, you have to be careful not to avoid doing church work and, thus, forget the Lord's work.

You have to have a "Mary and Martha" spirit.[6] Martha loved to serve Jesus, but Mary loved to worship Jesus. You have to be careful here, because you can neglect valuable family time and personal devotion time with God. You can become so busy working that you can easily forget to speak to people.

Martha's problem was a little different because she became discouraged when she felt she was not fully appreciated.

---

[6] Luke 10:38-42

Many times, servants, like Martha, have a problem with people serving them.

You've got to get excited about your gift!

I CANNOT BE STOPPED!

Numbers 23:20 (CEB)

Then Balaam raised his voice and made his address:
"Arise, Balak, and listen; hear me out, Zippor's son. God isn't a man
that he would lie, or a human being that he would change his mind.
Has he ever spoken and not done it, or promised and not fulfilled
it? I received a blessing, and he blessed. I can't take it back. He
hasn't envisioned misfortune for Jacob, nor has he seen trouble
for Israel. The LORD his God is with him, proclaimed as his king.
God, who brought them out of Egypt, is like
a magnificent wild bull for him

For as far back as I can remember, I have been a connoisseur of success. I have studied, researched, read, and listened to all kinds of materials and resources on what it takes to be blessed.

I particularly like watching biographies. I like reading the stories of great men and women because I want to know the pattern of the successful.

I had and still do have a whole shelf of books promising the secrets of success. Some say the secret is to have written goals. Some say to dress for success. Some advise on winning friends and influencing others. Some preach on ridding ourselves bad of habits, such as drinking too much and smoking. All of those things are good. And I did all those things. But then I looked back on all the things that I studied and the people that I researched, I found something very interesting.

You know those successful people I read about? They were people who drank and smoked and cursed. Many had no written goals. They had all types of bad habit. They didn't care about dressing well or looking the part.

But despite all their apparent flaws, they seemed to be happy internally. They were extremely successful and undeniably blessed. The only common denominator that I ever perceived one characteristic that seemed to tie them all together is that they had the relentless traits of a rhinoceros.

Like a rhinoceros, these men and women demonstrated a relentlessness, a tenacity in their approach to life. Whatever they did, they did it with a force in their hearts and a fire in their belly that says "I cannot be stopped."

And there are some lessons we can learn from the rhino that I believe are relevant to where we are now.

God's got MORE for me!

It's when you are blessed that you have to be most careful. The Bible said that after Joshua died, after having led the Children of Israel into the Promised Land, that another generation arose after them who did not know the Lord. They did not understand the work which He had done for the generation of Israelites that came before them. They did like most people do. They lived in their blessing and forgot that it was the Lord that had brought them out. They had gotten so used to the blessing that they forgot to praise the Giver of Blessings.

Deuteronomy 8:18 (CEB)

Remember the LORD your God! He's the one who gives you the strength to be prosperous in order to establish the covenant he made with your ancestors–and that's how things stand right now.

The word bless means to be enabled. When you realize that because of God's enablement and God's power, you are able to overcome. That means you are able to conquer any test, any trial, any circumstance or situation that comes up in your life because of God's power to help you and His ability to do in you what you could not do in your own strength.

One of the things that can happen when people see you blessed is that it can cause people to misjudge you. When they see you do things with God's strength behind you, they think that it is easier than it really is. But what they do not see is that quietly, and behind the scenes, God is pushing you, carrying you. And because you are not falling apart in a difficult situation or storm, people on the outside looking in will think that you are just strong, in your own strength. And they judge you.

Most people want to you to react to situations like they do and it creates a real problem in your relationships with others. Because when you get to this point, they won't help you or minister to you because they think you don't need anything. But what they don't understand is that beneath all of that strength is just a frail human being that has gotten to the place where you just depend upon God's strength to help you.

Have you ever surprised yourself and asked, "How did I make it through that?" Then you realized hat it was just God's strength that was maintaining you. Don't get it twisted! If you ever get that confused and think that is was your strength alone and not God helping you, you are setting yourself up for the greatest disappointment of your life.

The story of Samson terrifies me! He was an incredibly strong man – a man who had killed lions with his bare hands.

But one day, he found that his strength had left him. In Judges 16, we read that Delilah lulled him to sleep, then called out to the Philistines, who were upon him. Verse 20 continues, "He woke up from his sleep and thought, I will escape just like the other times and shake myself free. But he didn't realize that the LORD had left him." (CEB)

He tried to do what he used to do, but he did not recognize that his strength was gone. And thought he could always do what he always did without recognizing that God had stepped back for a moment to let him see that it was not he himself doing it, but it was the strength of God enabling him to do it.

David's prayer was, "Lord whatever you do, don't take your spirit from me." I know I messed up, but without you in my life I might as well be dead."

When the threat of the attack was great—too great for these people—when Balak was conjuring up what he was going to do, I'm sure he was saying, "Lord I don't want to be in this situation but if I am going to be in it I'm glad you are with me."

HE'S WITH YOU!!!

I noticed that the enemy knew who the people were. When you've got what you've got on you, you better know the enemy is well aware of who you are. The devil is a liar, and he's trying to prove that the test is greater than God's strength.

The test always looks BIGGER than God.

AT FIRST. But what you must remember is that God was in partnership with His people. If you could go and pull the rock out of Goliath's forehead you would notice that there is nothing exceptional about the rock. If you were to exhume David, if you were to raise him from the dead and look at his hands, there was nothing exceptional about David's hands. All he had was a slingshot, which is a child's toy. There was nothing exceptional about the instrument in David's hands that hurled the rock at Goliath. Yet Goliath fell to ground like lightning.

WHY? Because when David slung it with the strength of God. The power of God got behind the rock. And it was His power that pushed it through Goliath's head. If it were not for the enabling of God, the rock would have bounced off of Goliath's big head like a raindrop. And Goliath would have beaten David to death like a dog.

Many of you can relate to that. Nothing is exceptional about you. The reason you know that you are where you are is that God can take substandard equipment and perform supernatural feats. If it had not been for God on my side, the parakletos walking along side of me, my Goliath would not have fallen. Some people say, "I don't how I made it." But not me. I do know how I made it. I made it by the push of GOD.

Numbers 23:21 (CEB)

He hasn't envisioned misfortune for Jacob, nor has he seen trouble for Israel. The LORD his God is with him, proclaimed as his king.

Did you hear that? "The LORD his God is with him!" This is actually a cross reference to another passage about David.

Psalm 89:15-17 (CEB)

The people who know the celebratory shout are truly happy! They walk in the light of your presence, LORD! They rejoice in your name all day long and are uplifted by your righteousness because you are the splendor of their strength. By your favor you make us strong.

This leads me back to the next verse in Numbers 23.

Numbers 23:22 (CEB)

God, who brought them out of Egypt, is like a magnificent wild bull for him.

He compares them to a wild bull. Some translations say wild ox, which can also be translated RHINCEROS. He compares their deliverance to that of a rhino. You are not a cow, who cowers and runs away when things get tough, or who is satisfied grazing in the pasture. But not you. You've got rhinoceros skin! Two-inch thick rhinoceros skin. You are not scared, satisfied, or supersensitive. You're not running from your struggle; you're running towards it. You may be content, but you are never satisfied. You work with a singleness of purpose and vision and a relentless work ethic.

The reason that the rhinoceros is so dangerous is because they are not inclined to approach humans. They don't fool with people. But if people mess with them, that's an entirely different story! "Don't fool with me now! If you do, you've got hell on your hands!" Because once a rhino sets itself at charging at something, nothing can distract it. There is great power when you focus on one thing. The problem with some of you is that you spread yourself too thin.

I remember as a young boy, they were teaching us how to start a fire with a magnifying glass. And like most children, I liked playing with fire! I was so excited about trying it that I did not get all of the instructions. I had the magnifying glass. I had the paper. The sun was bright. But my fire would not start.

When I went back to class, I showed my teacher what I did. My teacher said, "You had all the elements correct." But he pointed out that I was moving the glass from spot to spot. The magnifying glass will not start a fire unless it is held in one spot continuously for a certain length of time.

This is why the enemy sends attacks to get you off of your spot. He knows that if you stay focused on your target, with the relentless charge and tenacity of a rhino, he's in trouble!

STAY FOCUSED

Jeremiah 17:8 (CEB)

They will be like trees planted by the streams, whose roots reach down to the water. They won't fear drought when it comes; their leaves will remain green. They won't be stressed in the time of drought or fail to bear fruit.

"Like a tree planted by the streams, I shall not be moved!"

Don't be moved by your distractors. Don't be swayed by a bad attitude (yours or someone else's!). Don't be blocked by your insecurities. And your opponents will think that when they attack you that they are burying you. They do not know you are planted here, with roots reaching down to the water.

And do you know what water often represents in scripture? It is a symbol of the Spirit of God! He's feeding me when I am hungry. He's nourishing me when I'm thirsty. I can come to the fountain, to the river, and drink!. And He won't be like some people, all dry and hateful. He said I can come to Him and drink and He will never run dry.

And like Shadrach, Meshach, and Abednego, you will not burn when heat comes. This is when you've reached another level; when you don't even see or feel or recognize their antics.

I AM PROSPEROUS!

The condition of the economy has nothing to do with you. Whether or not the people in your family are blessed has nothing to do with your blessing.

Numbers 23:22 (CEB)

God, who brought them out of Egypt,

is like a magnificent wild bull for him.

Just like sheep, rhinos have terrible eyesight. But they make up for it with a great sense of smell. A rhino's nose keeps it informed which animals are coming, which opportunities are nearby.

I SMELL VICTORY IN THE AIR!

I SMELL A BREAKTHROUGH!

I'VE GOT A FEELING SOMETHING BIG IS GETTING READY TO HAPPEN FOR ME.

Not only that, but they have a great sense of hearing. Along with its nose, a rhino's cup-shaped ears are very keen. If you are going to get your blessing, your hearing is going to have to be very sharp. You're going to have to hear what the Spirit of God is saying to the church. And faith comes by hearing, hearing the word of God.

And finally, rhinos have very sensitive feet. They can feel vibrations on the ground. And with a sense of audacity, this three-ton rhinoceros starts charging. Sometimes you can't see it, but you can feel it! Tell my dream I'm coming after it, full speed ahead. Tell my school I'm coming; full speed ahead. Tell my healing, tell the courts, tell every problem, every challenge, every task, I'm coming, full speed ahead! I'm going after every blessing that God has promised to me. I cannot be stopped. I've been through hell, but I cannot be stopped. And like a rhino, if you happen to get in my way, I'm afraid that the Holy Ghost in me might just run you over.

The only thing that the rhino can't do very well is to turn his head backwards. I'm not going back. I'm moving ahead. I'm here to declare that the past is over...

I'M A RHINO – I CANNOT BE STOPPED!

Lester Love is the Pastor of The City of Love. He possesses great leadership skills and is widely recognized for his ability to organize a team of people, energize them to accomplish any challenges that are set before them, and provide them with strategies for implementation. Born in Mississippi and raised in New Orleans, he joined Greater St. Stephen Full Gospel Baptist Church in 1980. He immediately began volunteering in ministry and eventually found his place as the First Assistant to his Pastor, Bishop Paul S. Morton, Sr. In 1997, Bishop Morton asked then Elder Love to serve as the Interim Pastor for a local church whose Pastor had fallen ill. Eventually, Love became the Senior Pastor of what is now The City of Love. In 2005, he was consecrated as the Bishop of Protocol for the Full Gospel Baptist Church Fellowship. In 2015, he was elevated to the office of Executive Secretary.

He travels across the country and abroad, presenting leadership sessions for other ministries and corporations. As a leader's leader, he has tapped into his gifts and developed the principles it takes to serve in excellence. His motivational mantra iCAN. **iWILL. iMUST!** encourages us to maximize our fullest potential.

Love has published several books including *Synergy: Staying Connected to Those Connected to You* and *Catching the Mantle: Positioned To Receive the Double Portion.* His first book, *The Art of Armor Bearing: God's Blueprint for Effective Servanthood*, quickly became the "how to" book for leadship and excellence in service training. His keynote addresses and workshops provide so many providential moments that attendees often follow-up with requests for one-on-one coaching.

Love's many talents include singing. He was the featured soloist on the CD "Where Love Abides," which won The Big Easy Award (New Orleans version of a Grammy) for Best Gospel Artist. He has also garnered national attention for his "Love Songs" clip on YouTube, which has surpassed 4 million views. He has served as the host of the Essence Music Festival Gospel Tribute for several years, the Merge Summit, the NBA All-Star Game and the Superbowl Gospel Celebration.

Lester and his wife Fran are the proud parents of three girls, Joy, Faith and Angel.